DISCERNMENT
SERIES

THE
JEZEBEL
SPIRIT

*Truths compiled
from the writings of*

FRANCIS
FRANGIPANE

UNMASKING
THE ENEMIES
OF THE CHURCH

Scripture taken from the New American Standard Bible
© 1960, 1962, 1963, 1968, 1971, 1972, 1973, 1975, 1977
by the Lockman Foundation. Used by permission.

ISBN #0-9629049-8-8

CONTENTS

chapters 1-4 from *The Three Battlegrounds*

INTRODUCTION

Over the years we have seen many of God's anointed ministers fall to the temptations of the Jezebel spirit. As the battle against this enemy rages, we feel the need to preface this study with a warning. Before presenting this topic to your congregation, it would be wise to teach about humility for a season. Humility will bring God's grace into your congregation and prepare a way of escape for all who are under the influence of this spirit. The individuals who are being assaulted by this enemy will then be able to receive help.

Our prayer is that each of us will not only be delivered from the reign of the Jezebel spirit, but inherit the morning star which Christ gives to those who overcome Jezebel.

1.

DISCERNING THE SPIRIT OF JEZEBEL

We are going to confront a strong-hold of immense proportions. It is a way of thinking that exists unchecked in most churches. We will expose, and then destroy, the hiding places of Jezebel.

Understanding the Spirit of Jezebel

"But I have this against you, that you tolerate the woman Jezebel, who calls herself a prophetess, and she teaches and leads My bond-servants astray, so that they commit acts of immorality and eat things sacrificed to idols" (Rev 2:20).

You may challenge my using this scripture and addressing it to American churches. You may argue that not one of the pastors you know has anyone who openly instructs people to commit acts of immorality. I understand your sense of alarm. I agree that you probably know of no one who brazenly preaches that sexual lust and idolatry are not sins. When we speak of Jezebel, we are identifying the source in our society of obsessive sensuality, unbridled witchcraft, and hatred for male authority.

To understand the spirit of Jezebel, we must understand the genesis of this personality in the Bible. The first mention of Jezebel is seen in the rebellious, manipulative wife of King Ahab. It was actually this spirit, operating through Queen Jezebel, which had caused over ten million Hebrews—all but seven thousand faithful souls—to bow to Baal. Jezebel caused them to forsake the covenant, destroy the sacred altars, and kill the prophets (see 1 Kings 19:14-18). This one spirit was almost totally responsible for corrupting an entire nation, and this principality has come full force against our nation.

Jezebel is fiercely independent and intensely ambitious for pre-eminence and control. It is noteworthy that the name "Jezebel," literally translated, means "without cohabitation." This simply means she refuses "to live together" or "cohabit" with anyone. Jezebel will not dwell with anyone unless she can control and dominate the relationship. When she seems submissive or "servant-like," it is only for the sake of gaining some strategic advantage. From her heart, she yields to no one.

Bear in mind that the spirit which produced Jezebel existed before its namesake was born. Although we refer to Jezebel as "she," this spirit is without gender. However, it is important to note that, while men in leadership are the main targets of most principalities, Jezebel is more attracted to the uniqueness of the female psyche in its sophisticated ability to manipulate without physical force.

Look for Jezebel to target women who are embittered against men, either through neglect or misuse of authority. This spirit operates through women who, because of insecurity, jealousy, or vanity, desire to dominate others. Jezebel is there behind the woman who publicly humiliates her husband with her tongue, and thereafter controls him by his fear of public embarrassment.

While she uses every means of sexual perversity known in hell, immorality is not the issue; *control* is what she seeks, using the power of sexual passions for the purpose of possessing men. To a woman under the influence of Jezebel, "conquering" a man need not involve physical contact if a seductive glance of her eyes will capture him.

The Battle Has Expanded

Since the era of the early apostles, and especially since the dawn of the electronic age, the scale of battle has greatly enlarged. It is difficult for us in our generation to discern the scope of warfare that hits the church and the world in general. We might actually suppose that warfare should decrease since the number of demons has not changed since the first century, while mankind has grown from three hundred million to over five billion souls today. Yet, the *access* the devil has to the souls in our world has increased through the mass communications media and literature. John wrote of this period in time in Revelation 12:15, **"And the serpent poured water like a river out of his mouth after the woman, so that he might cause her** [the church] **to be swept away with the flood."**

Water, in this context, symbolizes "words." In our world there exists a flood of *words* and *visual images* coming out of the mouth of Satan. Our society, through technological advances, has made sins of the mind and heart more accessible. More than ever before, the carnal mind, with its openness to this satanic flood of filth and rebellion, is being structured into a powerful stronghold for the devil.

In our information-filled, entertainment-oriented world, even minor demons can exercise major influence simply by possessing the script writers and producers of movies and television. Indeed, Satan has always been **"the prince of the power of the air"** (Eph 2:2). But we should realize that the **"power of the air"** is not merely the wind; we see that in our world this power uniquely includes the electronic airwaves which carry radio and television signals.

Therefore, we must discern exactly where the satanic inroads are in our own lives and cut them off. We cannot worship God on Sunday morning and then tolerate Jezebel through immoral entertainment in a movie Sunday night. Indeed, it is with this in mind that, in regard to warring against Jezebel, the eternal Word specifically described Himself as **"He who searches the *minds* and *hearts*"** (Rev 2:23), for it is in the inner sanctuary of our private soul-life where tolerance to Jezebel begins. It is here, within us, where tolerance must end.

Set the Captives Free!

Jezebel's spirit flows unhindered throughout the entertainment industries. This spirit flaunts itself in the world of fashion; it holds degrees in the philosophical departments of our schools and colleges. Where can you go in our society that the influence of the Jezebel spirit is not felt? She is the destroyer of politician and preacher alike. She is the cruel motivator behind abortion. It is Jezebel who engenders dissatisfaction between spouses.

This spirit was sitting in the church in Thyatira when it was exposed by the Holy Spirit nineteen hundred years ago (see Revelation 2:19-29). It still has its favorite seat in church. There are respectable men who love God and who seek to serve Him, yet secretly in their hearts are prisoners of Jezebel. Even now, they are deeply ashamed of their bondage to pornography, and they can barely control their desires for women. Ask them to pray and their spirits are awash with guilt and shame. Their prayers are but the whimpers of Jezebel's eunuchs.

There are good women who come to church seeking God, but this spirit has them fantasizing about the men in the assembly, lamenting that their husbands are not as "spiritual" as other husbands. Soon, these women develop problems that "only the pastor" can understand. Ladies, the **"older women"**—the *godly* women in the church—are the ones you need to consult with first, not pastor or elders (see Titus 2:3-5). If you must counsel with a church leader, do not be offended when he asks for his wife or an older, godly woman to join him.

Anyone who is hit by this spirit needs, first of all, to repent deeply of their sympathetic thoughts toward it, and then *war* against it! Do not waste days and weeks under condemnation. Separate yourself from that Jezebelian thinking which was fostered upon you in your youth, pick up the sword of the Spirit, and war against the principality of Jezebel! Pray for the saints in your church. Pray for the Christians throughout your community. *If you war against Jezebel when you are tempted, eventually you are going to become dangerous!* This spirit will stop attacking you once it recognizes that your aggressive counterattack is setting other people free!

Likely Targets

As we identify those whom this spirit will most likely influence, let us recognize that this demon can also operate through men. In fact, Jezebel seeks the highly refined qualities of the professional musician, especially when such a man has both the ambition and the opportunity to become a worship leader or director. It will also seek to surface in the pastor himself, in which case he will become very authoritarian and unyielding in his control of the church. Such a pastor will invariably be isolated from fellowship and accountability with other pastors. The man will find himself lured into maintaining flirtatious and sensual relationships, "special intimacies" with one or more women in the church. In time, he will most likely succumb to adultery.

Yet this spirit prefers the traits of a woman's nature. And since certain female ministries are more involved than others, it follows that they would be targets for the spirit of Jezebel. Church leaders should take heed. This spirit will seek to maneuver itself into leadership positions. Remember, Jesus said of Jezebel, "[she] **calls herself a prophetess**" (Rev 2:20). A woman can most certainly function prophetically; she can be anointed by God to serve in delegated authority as a prophetess. But when she insists upon recognition, when she manipulates or entirely disregards the male leadership in the church, *when she "calls herself a prophetess,"* beware.

Prayer leaders, church secretaries, worship and song leaders, pastors and wives, you are all especially targeted by this spirit. All of you serving in these roles should be instructed and warned about the warfare that may come against you. Each of you should be part of a church "warfare team" that is trained to war against Jezebel.

What Jezebel Hates

Jezebel's worst enemies are the prophets; her worst fear is that the people will embrace repentance. Jezebel hates repentance. Though this spirit will infiltrate the church, masking its desire for control with true Christian doctrines, it will hide from true repentance.

Jezebel hates humility. Jesus taught that greatness in the kingdom was not measured in what we seem to be, but in childlike honesty of heart. *A true ministry is willing and eager to be submitted and accountable to other ministries.* It is typical of those who are servant-minded. Therefore, we must learn that spirituality is measured in meekness, not power.

Jezebel hates prayer. Intercessory prayer pries her fingers off the hearts and souls of men. It sets people free in the spirit. When you pray, it binds her. When you pray against immorality, it cripples her. When you pray for a submissive heart, it is like the trampling of Jehu's horse upon her body.

Jezebel hates the prophets, for the prophets speak out against her. The prophets are her worst enemies. When she wars, it is to stir people against the message of the prophetic church. More than she hates the prophets, she hates the word they speak. Her real enemy is the spoken Word of God.

Jezebel's ultimate hatred is against God Himself. She hates the grace God lavishes upon His bondservants even after they sin. She hates the fact that God will take the weakest and lowliest and use them to bring her down. She hates the holiness and purity of heart that comes from God and surrounds those who serve in His courts.

Let's pray: *Father, we submit to You and Your standard of righteousness. We ask for purity, meekness, and holiness of heart. Forgive us for our tolerance of the spirit of Jezebel in both our minds and our deeds.*

Father, because we submit to You, we have Your authority to resist the devil. We bind, in the name of Jesus, the principality of Jezebel. We pull down the stronghold of its thinking over our community and our state. We come against the fortresses this demon has built up in the spirit realm in this area, and we release the Holy Spirit to plunder the house of Jezebel and distribute her goods.

We also speak faithfulness of eyes and heart to husbands and wives. We release purity of heart and grace to each member of the body of Christ, both single and married. We cover Your people with the blood of Jesus. We loose the joy of a humble and submissive spirit and pull down the imaginations of ambition and pride. In Jesus' name. Amen!

2.

ELIJAH, JEHU AND THE WAR AGAINST JEZEBEL

There is a war, a very ancient war, between the spirit of Elijah and the spirit of Jezebel. In this age-old battle, Elijah represents the interests of heaven: the call to repentance and the return to God. Jezebel, on the other hand, represents that unique principality whose purpose is to hinder and defeat the work of repentance.

To the Victor Goes Our Nation

To understand the conflict between the Elijah spirit and the spirit of Jezebel, we must understand these two adversaries as they are seen in the Scriptures. Each is the spiritual counterpart of the other. Is Elijah bold? Jezebel is brazen. Is Elijah ruthless toward evil? Jezebel is vicious toward righteousness. Does Elijah speak of the ways and words of God? Jezebel is full of systems of witchcraft and words of deceit. The war between Elijah and Jezebel continues today. The chief warriors on either side are the prophets of both foes; to the victor goes the soul of our nation.

In the tradition of Samuel, Elijah was the head of the school of prophets. Under him were the sons of the prophets—literally hundreds of seers and prophetic minstrels—who proclaimed the word of the Lord. In this war, however, Jezebel had viciously and systematically murdered all of God's servants until only Elijah remained (see 1 Kings 18:22). Elijah, as the last of the prophets, then challenged the 450 prophets of Baal and the 400 prophets of the Asherah to a demonstration of power: their gods against the power of the Lord.

These 850 men were the false prophets, the satanic priests **"who eat at Jezebel's table"** (1 Kings 18:19). They were the most powerful, demonized individuals that the hosts of darkness could produce. King Ahab, Jezebel's husband, sent a message out to **"all the sons of Israel,"** and the nation came to witness the conflict between the God of Elijah and the demigods of Jezebel.

The terms of the challenge were simple: each was to place an ox upon an altar. Elijah then said, **"you call on the name of your god, and I will call on the name of the Lord, and the God who answers by fire, He is God"** (1 Kings 18:24). Six hours later the cult priests still could produce no fire; twelve hours passed and Elijah began to mock them, **"Call out with a loud voice, for he is a god; either he is occupied or gone aside . . . perhaps he is asleep and needs to be awakened"** (v 27). Just before evening, Elijah prayed over his sacrifice and,

> **Then the fire of the Lord fell, and consumed the burnt offering . . . and when all the people saw it, they fell on their faces; and they said, "The Lord, He is God; the Lord, He is God"** (1 Kings 18:38-39).

Immediately after this powerful witness of the Lord, Elijah had the Hebrews hold the prophets of Baal and all of them were put to death.

We would suppose that, at this point, Elijah would have gone into Jezreel and asked God to finish off Jezebel, but he did not. In fact—and this may surprise you—Elijah came under spiritual warfare. Jezebel, in a fit of rage, released a flood of witchcraft and demonic power against Elijah that put fear into his heart. Elijah ran. You may ask, "How could such a mighty prophet turn and run?" The answer is not simple. In fact, the situation worsened. We then see Elijah sitting under a juniper tree, bewailing that he is no better than his fathers—actually praying that he might die! (see 1 Kings 19:4) What pressure overwhelmed this great man of God that he would fall prey to fear and discouragement? The spirit of Jezebel.

And now, let the reader understand. When you war against the principality of Jezebel, even though you stand against her lusts and witchcrafts, you must guard against the power demons of fear and discouragement; for these she will send against you to distract you from your warfare and your victory!

The Drama Continues . . .

It is an established principle in the spirit realm that one can impart a measure of the spirit-side of himself to another without the fullness of his own spirit diminishing. We see this when the spirit which was on Moses was placed upon the seventy elders (see Numbers 11:24-25; Deuteronomy 34:9). We can behold this in the process of the father's sins being passed on to the children (see Exodus 34:7). And, of course, we see this in Christ's Spirit dwelling within us. With this concept in mind, we can understand how the spirit of Elijah was sent to minister through the soul of John the Baptist.

Once before, Elijah's spirit had been placed upon another individual. You will remember that Elisha, the prophet who succeeded Elijah, received a double portion of Elijah's spirit (see 2 Kings 2:9-10). Now, again, the spirit of Elijah was ministering, activating, inspiring, and creating in John the Baptist that same kind of intensity which dwelt in Elijah himself. John was to go, **"as a fore-runner before Him** [the Lord] **in the spirit and power of Elijah"** (Luke 1:17). Jesus said of the Baptist, **"he himself is Elijah, who was to come"** (Matt 11:14, 17:11-13). John even looked like Elijah. He had returned; the spirit of Elijah was commissioned and sent into the world.

Like Elijah, John proclaimed the need for repentance wherever he saw sin. One such area was in the adulterous lives of King Herod and his wife, Herodias. When John confronted them, Herodias had him imprisoned (see Mark 6:19). But who was this, manipulating and controlling in the dark, spiritual side of Herodias? As Elijah's spirit ministered through John, so Jezebel had surfaced into this world through Herodias.

What Jezebel did to Elijah in the wilderness, Herodias now did to John; Jezebel hurled fear and discouragement, which leads to self-doubt and confusion, against the servant of God. John the Baptist, who had visibly seen the Spirit descend as a dove upon Christ, who heard God's audible voice bearing witness that Jesus was the Son of God, was now asking if Jesus truly was the Messiah, or should they look for another (see Matthew 11:3).

"And a strategic day came when Herod . . . gave a banquet" (Mark 6:21). "Strategic" is the perfect word to describe the timing of this event. For in this war between the spirits of Elijah and Jezebel, Herodias had her daughter dance before Herod, enticing out of him a promise to give whatever she asked. At her mother's request—more truly, at *Jezebel's* request —she demanded the head of the Baptist. And temporarily, the confrontation between the spirits of these two eternal enemies subsided.

Elijah is Coming!

Two thousand years ago, Jesus stated that the ministry of Elijah was not over. He promised, **"Elijah is coming and will restore all things"** (Matt 17:11). Malachi the prophet also wrote, **"Behold, I am going to send you Elijah the prophet before the coming of the great and terrible day of the Lord. And he will restore"** (Mal 4:5-6). Elijah IS coming to war and restore! He came before the Great Day and he is returning before the Terrible Day of the Lord!

Remember, however, the principle mentioned earlier: one can impart a measure of the spirit-side of himself to another without the fullness of his own spirit diminishing. *Today, even as God did with Elijah, Elisha, and John the Baptist, the Lord is raising up an Elijah company of prophets: Spirit-filled men and women sent forth to prepare the way for the return of Christ!*

Let it also be known that, if Elijah is coming before Jesus returns, so also is Jezebel. Indeed, do you not see her in our land in the abundance of witchcraft and harlotries? Do you not hear her brazen voice rejecting God's authority and exalting her rebellion in feminism? Have you not beheld her causing even God's **"bond-servants"** to **"commit acts of immorality"**? (Rev 2:20) Seeing Jezebel so blatantly manifest herself only confirms that the spirit of Elijah is also here bringing repentance and raising up warring prophets throughout our land! In fact, if you are going to serve God during the reign of a "Jezebel," the warfare itself will thrust you into a prophetic anointing simply that you may survive!

In the Old Testament we see how God destroyed Jezebel. Jehu, the newly crowned king of Israel, was sent by the word of the Lord through Elijah's successor, Elisha, to fulfill God's promise. As Jehu and his men furiously drove their chariots toward Jezreel, the kings of Israel and Judah came out to meet him.

"Is it peace, Jehu?" And he answered, "What peace, so long as the harlotries of your mother Jezebel and her witchcrafts are so many?" (2 Kings 9:22)

And Jehu slew the two kings. Immediately afterward, he rode into Jezreel to confront Jezebel. The Word tells us that when she saw him, she painted her eyes and adorned her head, and looking out an upper window, she called to him,

"Is it well, Zimri [Jehu], **your master's murderer?" Then he lifted up his face to the window and said, "Who is on my side? Who?" And two or three officials** [eunuchs] **looked down at him. And he said, "Throw her down." So they threw her down, and some of her blood was sprinkled on the wall and on the horses, and he trampled her under foot** (2 Kings 9:31-33).

There was something in Jehu's spirit that we must possess today in our war against Jezebel. While we must be compassionate toward those captured by Jezebel, Jehu had no mercy, no hope for reform, no compromise or sympathy whatsoever toward this demonic spirit! Jehu **"trampled her under foot."** While she lay bleeding and near death, he trampled her beneath the feet of his horse!

So also with us, we must have no tolerance whatsoever for this spirit! *There can be no peace, no relaxing under our "fig tree," until Jezebel is slain!* We must stop living for comfort as long as her harlotries and witchcrafts are so many in our land! We must refuse to settle for a false peace based on compromise and fear, especially when the Spirit of God is calling for "War"!

It is significant that the *eunuchs* cast her down. Some of you who are reading this have been made eunuchs: slaves to this evil spirit. Today, right now, God is giving you the privilege of participating in the eternal judgment against Jezebel. *You* cast her down! Side with God, and let the judgments of God come forth!

It is time for the prophets to unite against this spirit! Under the anointing of Elijah, in the power of the Holy Spirit, let us arise in the indignation of Jehu and cast Jezebel down! Even now, we wash ourselves in the Precious Blood, and having been cleansed from any defilement of sin, we shatter and plunder the stronghold of Jezebel!

Pray with us: *Spirit of Jezebel, in the authority of Jesus Christ, which He gives us as His servants, we release your captives! We set free your slaves! We speak to the eunuchs, cast down your sympathetic strongholds toward Jezebel! Cast down her evil imaginations from your minds! In the power of Jesus' name, we release you from her psychic grip upon your soul. In the authority of the living Christ, we proclaim HOLY WAR upon the spirit of Jezebel! Amen.*

3.

OUR EXPERIENCE WITH JEZEBEL

What we present to you comes from our experience. We offer you no theories, no speculations. What we share with you has worked.

To Deliver, We Ourselves Must Be Delivered

"He will deliver one who is not innocent, and he will be delivered through the cleanness of your hands" (Job 22:30). There is a difference between repenting for a sin and actually pulling down the stronghold within us that produced the sin. The first involves faith in the cross of Christ; the second demands we embrace crucifixion ourselves. In this regard, in 1971 the Lord began a foundational work of cleansing my heart from the influence of the Jezebel spirit.

This season of repentance lasted about forty days. During that time, through the Holy Spirit, the stronghold which was tolerant toward the spirit of Jezebel was pulled down. I should make it clear that I was not repenting again for sins previously washed and forgiven. As was stated earlier, my repentance was not for sins, but for the *nature* that caused my sins. This is the essence of pulling down strongholds: We destroy the defiling, oppressive *system of thinking* which, through the years, has been built into our nature. My goal was simply that I be renewed in **"the spirit of** [my] **mind"** (Eph 4:23).

The manner in which this happened was as follows: The Holy Spirit brought to mind many of the sins from my unsaved youth. Two or three times a day, every day, in dreams or as I worked, the Lord brought past events to my mind. As the Lord revealed these incidents, I covered each memory with the blood of Jesus. Each time I prayed, I knew that through the Spirit another "stone" was being removed from this fortress in my mind.

Finally, the Lord revealed through a dream that this stronghold had been pulled down. In the dream two men were talking, one of whom was holding a baby.

The one holding the child used a vile word in his conversation. Suddenly embarrassed because of the infant, he quickly reassured himself that the baby was so innocent that it did not know the meaning of the word. In the dream, I realized that *I* also did not know the meaning of this word; in this, the grace of God had brought a new innocence into my heart, of which the baby in the dream was a symbol. At that time, I knew nothing of the spirit of Jezebel. Nevertheless, the Lord was building in me a measure of immunity against it.

Our First Encounter with Jezebel

During the 1970s, I pastored in an organization which had scores of men who functioned in the revelation gifts of wisdom and knowledge. There was "day and night" prayer, beautiful worship, commitment, and power. As the Lord was to Jacob on the plains of Moab, so He was also to us like the horns of the wild ox (see Numbers 23:22). There seemed no curse or omen that worked against us; God had given us His blessing, and success seemed inevitable. But as Balaam counselled Balak to seduce the Israelites with the daughters of Moab, so the spirit of Jezebel launched its attack upon this work of God.

If the enemy cannot attack you directly, he will seek to bring you into sin, thereby positioning you under the judgments of God. When the Jezebel spirit began to manifest itself and tolerance toward sexual sins increased, I approached the founder of the movement with my concerns. Meeting with him privately, I entreated him as a son does a father; but he dismissed me. Three months later I approached him again, appealing this time to the entire governmental team which was with him, warning them with tears that the judgment of the Lord against tolerating Jezebel was sickness and death (see Revelation 2:22-23). Once more I was dismissed. Several months later I was removed from leadership and then, ultimately, forced from the group. Within months after I left, the leader divorced his wife, and less than a year later he married his secretary. Within two years he was dead from prostate cancer.

The impact of this experience was both devastating and enlightening. Even though I personally went through a period of great discouragement and self-doubt, I learned much about Jezebel and the sin of presumption. I saw that when men assume God will not judge them, it is only a matter of time before the tempter comes to destroy them. It is significant that, while Jesus had the gifts of wisdom and understanding, counsel, strength, and knowledge, His *delight* was **"in the fear of the Lord"** (Isa 11:2-3). The sin of presumption is the antithesis of the fear of the Lord. It is the harbinger of future defeat.

Releasing Souls Through Prayer

That was our first experience with the spirit of Jezebel, though not the last. In 1985, during a time of counselling, we discerned that this spirit was the controlling influence, directing the lesser demons of homosexuality and lesbianism. The Lord instructed us to war against Jezebel, and in one month's time three people were delivered from these perversions! The next month the local cable network removed the Playboy channel. People needing deliverance from sexual fantasies began calling us for help. Even pastors and their wives, without knowing we were doing warfare, were calling to confess sins and receive deliverance. By focusing our warfare against this Jezebel, many in her grip were being set free!

At the same time, the warfare increased considerably against both my family and our church. A demon named "Faultfinder" (which we did not discern until months later) brought division and conflict into the congregation. Certain people, whom we loved deeply, suddenly turned against us with unexplained hatred. Suspicion mounted in the church and a time of destabilization occurred. Nevertheless, we continued warring against this spirit, convinced our warfare was effective.

One night, however, the spirit of Jezebel appeared at the foot of our bed. I felt paralyzed, unable to speak or even cry for help. This spirit, which had alienated even our close friends, was now standing before me, unfiltered by a human body. I felt as if all life had been literally drained from my body—that only Christ's life sustained me.

No audible words were spoken, but this principality put the following words into my mind, *"Continue to pray as you are, and I will kill you and the members of your church."* The spirit faded, but even after it had apparently left, I was barely able to move. My mind was a quagmire of discouraging thoughts: "Why should I pray for these people? Why suffer when, on any given day, I don't know who will be turned against me?" Eventually, the Holy Spirit intervened, and the oppression broke.

But Jezebel's death threat was not idle. Less than a week later, a woman in the church called asking for help. Her husband had taken drugs and was threatening her and her children. We made provisions for her, and she and her youngsters escaped. At 1 a.m. that same night, I received a phone call from her enraged husband. This man, a self-styled Nazi and owner of thirty-four guns, was demanding I tell him where his wife was. He said, "If you don't tell me where my wife is, *I will kill you and the members of your church!"* These were the exact words the spirit of Jezebel had used in my bedroom less than one week earlier! It was obvious that the Jezebel spirit had found and raised up a vessel to carry out the death threat of the previous week.

It is not normal practice for pastors to pray *for* a snowstorm on a Saturday night, but we prayed that night, and the light snow falling outside turned into a blizzard, dropping ten inches of snow by church time Sunday morning. The few of us who did come to church prayed again and bound Jezebel from the man who had threatened us. Eventually, to God's glory, this individual accepted the Lord as his Savior.

This has been a summary of our experience with the spirit of Jezebel. If you witness to the reality of our message, then pray about your involvement in fighting this principality. What we have written is not based upon theory or conjecture, but experience. Our testimony in this warfare is simply this: The Lord Jesus Himself has given us His authority **"over all the power of the enemy."** His promise is faithful: *"and nothing shall injure you"* (Luke 10:19).

4.

STRATEGY AGAINST THE SPIRIT OF JEZEBEL

You cannot defeat the enemy simply with prayer. To topple Satan's empire, we must be transformed into Christ's likeness.

Our War Against Jezebel

The church that successfully wars against Jezebel will be a church that inherits the glorious **"morning star,"** which will be a visible outward glory, a symbol of hidden, inward purity. It will be a church that exercises **"authority over the nations,"** uniquely, because it has conquered the Jezebel spirit which sought to strip God's servants of authority. It will be a church in which the gift of healing is an integral part of their body ministry (see Revelation 2:26-28).

There are great prizes in winning the war against Jezebel. Although every victory is initiated by prayer, the rewards of God will not be attained only through intercession. As we have stated, victory begins with the name of Jesus on our lips. But it is not consummated until the nature of Jesus is in our hearts.

Therefore, in regard to our war against Jezebel, we must allow the Holy Spirit to expose where we are tolerant and sympathetic to the ways of this evil spirit. *We cannot be successful in the heavenly war if we are not victorious in the battlefield of our minds.* There is only one realm of final victory against the enemy: Christlikeness.

Jesus is **"He who searches the minds and hearts"** (Rev 2:23). Our victory in every battle begins here, in our **"minds and hearts."** Consequently, we cannot tolerate Jezebelian thinking in any area. Our concept of church must expand beyond buildings into a way of life we practice everywhere. Since *we* are the church, let us realize that we are still in the church when we are home. When we turn on television to an immoral program, we are still in the church, tolerating the spirit of Jezebel.

If a husband is afraid of his strong-willed wife or unable to serve as the head of his household, although he is not in the worship building, he is still in the church tolerating Jezebel. Our time spent in the worship service is necessary, but it is a very small part of our continuing church life. It is in the routine things of daily living where the strongholds of Jezebel must be confronted and destroyed.

It Takes an "Ahab" to Tolerate Jezebel

There is a spirit which works with Jezebel. The effect of this demon is that it floods the soul of a man with weakness and fear. Its name is Ahab; his nature is "one who *gives* his authority to Jezebel."

The Ahab spirit occupies the areas of tolerance within a man's mind. The man feels almost drugged in his struggle against Jezebel. To win against Jezebel, one must conquer the nature of Ahab.

The man who is married to a domineering wife will exhibit one of two responses: He will either be fearful in other relationships in his life or he will tend to resent women in general. If he is an employer, he will be overly harsh and control-oriented toward females, quick to put them "in their place." This is a manifestation of his resentment toward his wife.

The essence of Ahab's nature is to have a title, "husband," and a position, "head," but never truly exercise spiritual authority. When Ahab was king, Jezebel ruled. The man who cannot govern his household in godly, protective authority will not exercise his spiritual authority elsewhere. Such a man needs to repent of his fears and firmly, with gentleness, set his home in order.

But let us further clarify authority. Authority is simply delegated responsibility. The emphasis is not on being the boss, but being responsible. The substructure upon which divine authority comes forth is divine love. Headship in the home is simply the man taking loving responsibility for the condition of his family. No man will have peace in his home if he views authority as simply the domination of his wife. God's will is to have couples making decisions together, each drawing upon the wisdom of the other, enjoying themselves as friends in open and loving communion.

God's answer to dealing with Jezebel is not to exchange one form of oppression (Jezebel's), for another (the man's). God's objective is to replace Jezebel's concept of security with the security a woman receives when she is tenderly loved by her husband. Thus, the man wins the war against Jezebel by becoming Christlike.

The woman overcomes the haughtiness of Jezebel by seeking the meekness of Christ. She pursues a **"gentle and quiet spirit"** (1 Peter 2:23-3:4), which is natural to Christlikeness. The woman must see God's wisdom in the divine order of the family and honor her husband as her head. If she is unmarried, she should be submitted to the order God has established in her church as unto the Lord. Her humility and peace in serving others is a sign of destruction to the nature of Jezebel (see Philippians 1:28).

The woman conquers the sensual side of Jezebel by renouncing her feminine charms, which are **"deceitful"** (Prov 31:30), and her **"many persuasions"** (Prov 7:21), which are enticing. She refuses the sensual look of the eyes and seductive softening of the voice. If she is married, her beauty is given to her husband. If she is single, she adorns her inner person with the spiritual qualities of the fruit of the Spirit, knowing that if she compromises her standards with God, she will inevitably find a man who will compromise his standards with her. The true man God has for her is a godly man in search of a virtuous woman. Her victory begins with prayer, but it is consummated by transformation.

What we become in Christ, *as His people,* must be the exact opposite of the spirit of Jezebel. Is she rebellious? We must become submissive. Is she proud and haughty? We must become meek and lowly of heart. Is she a control demon?

We must be gentle and willing to yield. Does Jezebel send forth witchcraft and immorality, fear, and discouragement? We must live a crucified life in the purity of Christ, full of love and faith for our vision. Again, it is Who Christ becomes in us that establishes our victory against the spirit of Jezebel.

Corporate Warfare Against Satan's Powers

"And . . . they lifted their voices to God with one accord" (Acts 4:24). As important as it is to win the war against Jezebel in the home, we must also join together for corporate prayer and warfare. Corporate prayer is the united intercession of the church against the powers of darkness. This type of warfare can be accomplished with a great variety of expression and with a minimum of requirements. Nevertheless, those requirements are essential to effective warfare.

1. Worship Should Be Part of Warfare.

With great variety, worship and praise should be integrated into warfare. During our warfare, various individuals spontaneously will lead out with appropriate songs. Keep your eyes on Jesus and stay thankful!

2. Intercession Should Be Spirit-Led.

This means more than "praying in tongues." It requires that we learn to listen. Often, corporate prayer is actually hindered by someone dominating the group with loud, insensitive "tongues." When you pray corporately, there is a *common fountain* from which those who pray must draw. It requires that we be responsive to the subtle changes of the Spirit as He guides the group into creative agreement. As individuals we seek to keep our prayers short (2 to 5 minutes); we address one need at a time, leaving the door open for others to pray in agreement.

3. Seek to Remain Consistent to Scheduled Prayer Times.

This may sound like we are seeking to control the Holy Spirit; but the more predictable the schedule, the more people can commit themselves to it. However, stay open for those special seasons when the Lord calls for additional intercession.

4. Do Not Become Presumptuous.

In fact, if someone resorts to calling the devil names, "daring him to fight," etc., instruct him that he is out of order. In prayer, use the Word, the Spirit, and the Name of Jesus; anything more is fleshly.

5. Keep All Talk to a Minimum.

Save all but essential conversation for after the prayer time.

6. Those Who Engage in Warfare Should be Trained and Approved by Church Leadership.

It would be wise to have a "warfare team" as well as a "backup team" which prays for those on the front lines. The backup team should consist of those in training or those who feel called only to pray.

5.

FREE TO LAUGH

The Jezebel spirit is Satan's answer for a woman's protection in a harsh, male-dominated world.

Godliness or Witchcraft

The Jezebel spirit exploits the offenses a woman may have received from ungodly men, forcing the woman to utilize manipulation, sensuality, and intimidation to make her way through life. Yet, it drives the woman beyond mere survival, developing her more intuitive nature until, whether she realizes it or not, the techniques she applies to personal relationships are akin to principles of witchcraft.

The entry of this spirit into the woman's life is full of irony. The woman, in her rebellion from the harsh, unloving demands of corrupted male authority, finds shelter and strength in becoming like her oppressor. *She herself becomes harsh and unloving.* Thus, the very thing she hated in men, she has now become.

The defense God offers for women, however, is the nature of Christ. Indeed, the antidote for the Jezebel spirit is Jesus' humility. His call to us requires that we crucify our "rights" and put our list of things which have offended us upon the cross. Thus, Christ makes all things new. Because we follow Him, we forgive those who have hurt us and love those who were our enemies. The effect of Christ's love not only offers hope for our antagonists, but is a source of protection, a buffer, between us and the harshness of life. Indeed, through the way of Christ we not only find protection but eternal life. We can become fruitful in the land of our affliction.

Deliverance of Spirit and Soul

We know many women who once were in bondage to the Jezebel spirit but now have been delivered from its ways. These are women who function today in respected ministries throughout the nation. They no longer feel they must become manlike to have ministries; they are feminine and glorify Christ in their womanhood.

The Jezebel spirit, however, is a perverse spirit which seeks to alter women

into men and to make men into women.
Since the Jezebel spirit offers an "illegal" strength to the woman, her deliverance will not begin until she can embrace a transition time of weakness. As Christ was crucified **"because of weakness,"** yet He lives **"because of the power of God"** (2 Cor 13:4), so God will work dependency into the woman's heart until she trusts in the power and goodness of God for her security, not in her manipulation of people.

The Jezebel stronghold is rooted in the woman's reactions to fear. She controls because she seeks predictability; she manipulates because she cannot trust. However, the scriptures tell us that **"perfect love casteth out fear: because fear hath torment"** (1 John 4:18 KJV). During the process of deliverance, she needs godly men and women to stand with her in love, especially as she embraces the allotted times of weakness. Remember, the woman under the influence of this spirit is a woman tormented. She has not been properly loved; the Jezebel stronghold is the result.

Those who work to help such individuals should acknowledge with thankfulness that the woman who has come for help has already taken the first step toward her deliverance: she recognizes her need. You must confirm to her your commitment to this process of deliverance.

There will be stages in her deliverance; the deliverance of the soul is different than the liberation of the woman's spirit. The soul is made of life's events: the memories and hopes, loves and hates, experiences and reactions. It is your personality, intellect, and emotions. Your spirit, however, is the silent observer when you dream; it is the evaluator of your thoughts. As it is written, **"Who among men knows the thoughts of a man except the spirit of the man, which is in him?"** (1 Cor 2:11)

The *spirit* of the woman must be delivered first. In her innermost being she must recognize the difference between her hard, Jezebelian thoughts and the softness of Christ's way of life. She must identify in her spirit that subtle shift that moves from trusting God to anxiously manipulating other people. Once she receives deliverance in her spirit, she can proceed with deliverance in her soul.

The *soul* must experience renewal in the mind; that is, the full range of the individual's thought-life must be cleansed and retrained according to the word of God. This process takes longer than the initial awakening of the individual's spirit and its subsequent deliverance.

In the process of the soul's deliverance, we should recognize that thoughts have their own self-life; they are sustained by our willingness to accept them. No thought or idea graciously accepts death. Thus, thoughts must be taken **"captive to** the **obedience of Christ"** (2 Cor 10:5), through which strongholds in the mind are pulled down.

The individual is well on the road to victory when, instead of becoming insecure when old Jezebel-like patterns emerge, she remains calm, even laughing at the way she used to react. She confidently abides in the peace and character of the Lord Jesus Christ.